THIS or THAT?

BOOK 1

Brandon T. Snider

STERLING CHILDREN'S BOOKS
New York

D0711655

STERLING CHILDREN'S BOOKS
New York

An Imprint of Sterling Publishing Co., Inc.
1166 Avenue of the Americas
New York, NY 10036

STERLING CHILDREN'S BOOKS and the distinctive Sterling Children's Books logo are registered trademarks of Sterling Publishing Co., Inc.

©2016 by Sterling Publishing Co., Inc.

All images by depositphotos, iStockphoto, and Shutterstock with the following exception: © Marta Nardini/Getty Images (boy with banana)

All rights reserved. No part of this publication may be reproduced, stored in a retrieval system, or transmitted in any form or by any means (including electronic, mechanical, photocopying, recording, or otherwise) without prior written permission from the publisher.

ISBN 978-1-4549-2102-8

Distributed in Canada by Sterling Publishing Co., Inc.
C/o Canadian Manda Group, 664 Annette Street
Toronto, Ontario, Canada M6S 2C8
Distributed in the United Kingdom by GMC Distribution Services
Castle Place, 166 High Street, Lewes, East Sussex, England BN7 1XU
Distributed in Australia by NewSouth Books, 45 Beach Street,
Coogee, NSW 2034, Australia

For information about custom editions, special sales,
and premium and corporate purchases, please contact Sterling Special Sales
at 800-805-5489 or specialsales@sterlingpublishing.com.

Manufactured in China

Lot #:
2 4 6 8 10 9 7 5 3 1
10/16

www.sterlingpublishing.com

Cover and interior design by Philip T. Buchanan

WOULD YOU RATHER

drink a glass of
pancake batter

or

eat a
raw sausage
pizza?

WOULD YOU RATHER
have one big zit on your nose

or

lots of
little **ZITS**
covering
your face?

WOULD YOU RATHER
have a small birthday party
with your closest friends

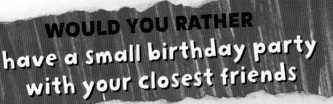

or

have a giant
birthday
bash with
hundreds of
strangers?

WOULD YOU RATHER

drink a glass
of nacho cheese

swim in cold
CHICKEN
SOUP?

WOULD YOU RATHER
find out your dad is the
king of an **ELF KINGDOM**

or

find out
you're a
VAMPIRE?

**WOULD
YOU RATHER**

sleep in a mud
puddle for
one night

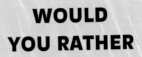

sleep in an
empty field in
the middle of
nowhere for
one night?

WOULD YOU RATHER

play a crazy prank on your MOM

or

play a crazy prank on your DAD?

WOULD YOU RATHER
squeal like a pig whenever you're really happy

or

cry like a baby whenever you don't get your way?

**WOULD
YOU RATHER**
take your crush
to a dance, but
they laugh at
you behind
your back

take a close friend
who secretly has a crush
on you, but you don't
feel the same way?

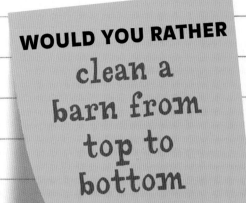

WOULD YOU RATHER

clean a
barn from
top to
bottom

or

massage a cow's
udder for one
hour?

WOULD YOU RATHER have a big booger hanging out of your nose

or

toilet paper hanging out of your pant leg?

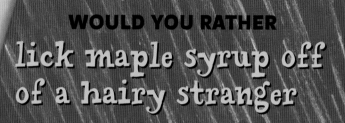

WOULD YOU RATHER
lick maple syrup off of a hairy stranger

or

eat year-old yogurt out of your best friend's armpit?

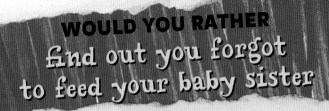

WOULD YOU RATHER
find out you forgot
to feed your baby sister

or

find out
you forgot
to wear
underwear?

WOULD YOU RATHER

Sing your favorite song
in front of a stadium
FULL OF PEOPLE

or

Sing a song
that you absolutely
hate in front of your
ENTIRE CLASS?

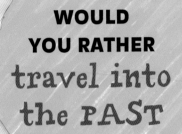

WOULD YOU RATHER travel into the PAST

or

travel into the FUTURE?

WOULD YOU RATHER
spend an entire day
with someone who
dislikes you

change all your
social media
profile pictures
to one of you
posing with
someone you
dislike?

WOULD YOU RATHER

stop washing
your hair

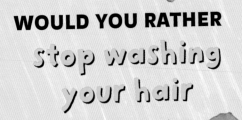

or

stop
wiping your
butt?

**WOULD
YOU RATHER**

stick your
hand in pee

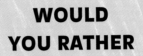

or

chew a piece
of liver for
two hours?

WOULD YOU RATHER spend the night by yourself in a dark, abandoned warehouse

or

spend the night in a house filled with strangers?

WOULD YOU RATHER
blow your nose with sandpaper

or

take a bath
in vegetable
soup?

WOULD YOU RATHER
have one extremely long nose hair you can't cut

or

no hair on your body at all?

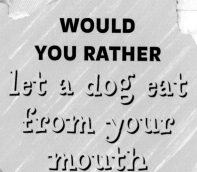

WOULD YOU RATHER *let a dog eat from your mouth*

or

let a cat lick you clean?

WOULD YOU RATHER

show up at a regular party dressed as a fairy princess zombie vampire

show up at a costume party where you know no one and are only wearing a long T-shirt?

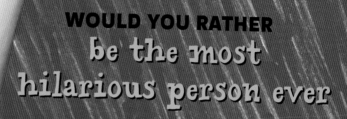

WOULD YOU RATHER
be the most
hilarious person ever

be best friends
with the most
hilarious
person ever?

WOULD YOU RATHER

climb a
mountain
blindfolded

ride a scary
roller coaster for
five hours?

WOULD YOU RATHER
drink a gallon of GARBAGE JUICE

or

eat a softball-size clump of DOG HAIR?

WOULD YOU RATHER

flash your belly
at a stranger

or

go to a party
by yourself?

WOULD YOU RATHER

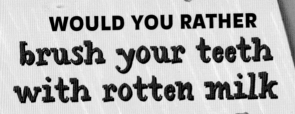

brush your teeth
with rotten milk

take a bath
in salad
dressing?

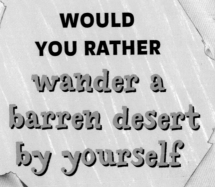

**WOULD
YOU RATHER**

wander a
barren desert
by yourself

get lost in a
dangerous jungle
with a friend?

WOULD YOU RATHER have a fancy dinner with your crush

or

have a light snack with an intriguing stranger?

WOULD YOU RATHER
tell a very bad joke to a big audience that boos

or

accidentally trip and fall down onstage?

WOULD YOU RATHER draw blue freckles all over your face

or

wear a bright-orange wig for a month?

WOULD YOU RATHER

tell someone you
love that you
hate them

tell someone
you hate
that you
love them?

WOULD YOU RATHER

get caught cheating by your teacher

tell your parents you cheated and that you regret it?

WOULD YOU RATHER
moon your teacher

or

stick your
tongue
out at a
police officer?

WOULD YOU RATHER be covered in HAIR

or

covered in FRECKLES?

WOULD YOU RATHER

have a cool
boss at
a job you
DISLIKE

a mean boss at a job
you **LOVE?**

WOULD YOU RATHER

parachute out of a plane

or

dive
to the
darkest
depths of
the sea?

WOULD YOU RATHER

have your brain transferred into the body of a funny chimpanzee

into the body of an evil spider?

WOULD YOU RATHER

talk to a stranger
for an hour

or

talk to your
best friend using only
hand signals for
two hours?

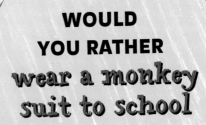

WOULD YOU RATHER wear a monkey suit to school

or

wear a baby's diaper to a party?

WOULD YOU RATHER

eat a raw onion soaked in butter

or

drink a hamburger smoothie?

WOULD YOU RATHER
give a creepy stranger
a back rub

or

eat a
small
snake egg?

WOULD YOU RATHER find out you have a SECRET TWIN

or

find out your mom is a ROBOT SPY?

**WOULD
YOU RATHER**
be able to burp
your ABCs

or

have the
ability to fart
 10
times in
a row?

WOULD YOU RATHER

lose all
of your
HAIR

lose all of
your
TEETH?

WOULD YOU RATHER
sit in a closet for an hour
with a big piece of dog poop

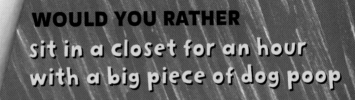

or

with a cup
of warm vomit?

WOULD YOU RATHER never do your favorite thing again

or

do your least favorite thing every day for one year straight?

WOULD YOU RATHER

keep a dead fish in your backpack for a week

or

carry around a box filled with dead insects for a month?

WOULD YOU RATHER have eyebrows that are five inches long

or

two football-size ears?

WOULD YOU RATHER

eat a spoonful of dead skin

a spoonful of toenail clippings?

WOULD YOU RATHER

people called you
WEAK

or

called you
FEARFUL?

**WOULD
YOU RATHER
eat a peanut-
butter-and-bologna
sandwich**

or

**a smoothie
made with
fruit punch
and squid?**

wake up to find you have zero presents on Christmas

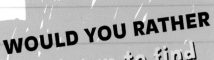

or

wake up to find you have one present that you can't keep?

WOULD YOU RATHER
forget your entire
history up 'til now

or

be told
the exact
moment
you'll die?

WOULD YOU RATHER

be trapped in a coffin for five hours

or

stand naked in the freezing rain for two hours?

WOULD YOU RATHER
live in a world
without
CARS

live in
a world
without
MOVIES?

WOULD YOU RATHER teach someone a simple magic trick

learn a very complicated magic trick that you can never show anyone?

WOULD YOU RATHER

be SWEATY
all the time

or

have dry,
FLAKY
skin?

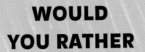

WOULD YOU RATHER
be SCARED all the time

or

SAD all the time?

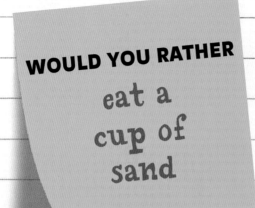

WOULD YOU RATHER

eat a
cup of
sand

or

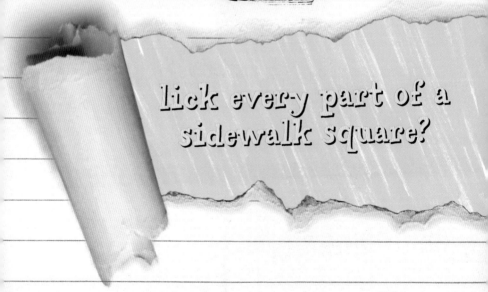

lick every part of a
sidewalk square?

have nails like a hawk's talons

or

a face
like a
beaver's?

WOULD YOU RATHER

swim in a crystal-clear, icy lake

dip your leg into a deep, murky pond for ten minutes?

WOULD YOU RATHER
lose an **EYEBALL**
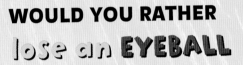

or

have only one
NOSTRIL?

WOULD YOU RATHER

surf in shark-infested waters

or

hike in a forest filled with bears?

WOULD YOU RATHER
be sprayed by a
SKUNK

or

soak in a
tub filled with
DEAD FISH?

WOULD YOU RATHER
tell your best friend a **BIG LIE**

or

tell your
best friend a
**HARSH
TRUTH?**

WOULD YOU RATHER walk around for a day dressed as a **CLOWN**

or

wearing pants filled with **TINY TURTLES?**

WOULD YOU RATHER
have a head that's
three times bigger
than normal

one
really
muscly leg?

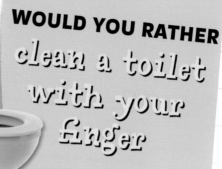

WOULD YOU RATHER
clean a toilet with your finger

or

discuss a very sensitive subject with your mom?

WOULD YOU RATHER

eat a thimble of DANDRUFF

or

drink a
teaspoon of
BLOOD?

WOULD YOU RATHER go on a luxury vacation with a ninety-year-old grandpa

or

with a two-month-old baby?

WOULD YOU RATHER

do a nice thing to a mean person

or

a mean thing to a nice person?

WOULD YOU RATHER
feel like you're about to
SNEEZE for one hour

have the
HICCUPS
for two
hours?

WOULD YOU RATHER
carry a cuddly teddy bear around with you until you're twenty years old

or

carry a snake around with you for one year?

WOULD YOU RATHER

wake up in your
GRANDMA'S BODY

or

in the
body of a
STRANGER?

WOULD YOU RATHER *marry an* **ALIEN WARLORD**

or

marry a very MEAN TEACHER?

WOULD YOU RATHER

take a shower
with an angry
raccoon

or

stick your hand
into a giant fish tank
containing a
single piranha?

WOULD YOU RATHER
be accused of STEALING

or

of LYING?

WOULD YOU RATHER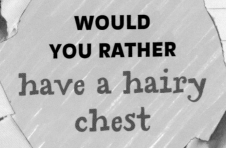
have a hairy chest

or

a hairy back?

WOULD YOU RATHER
eat your food in pellet form

as a tall glass of creamy liquid?

WOULD YOU RATHER

make a
bully mad

defend a bully
when someone is
making fun of
them?

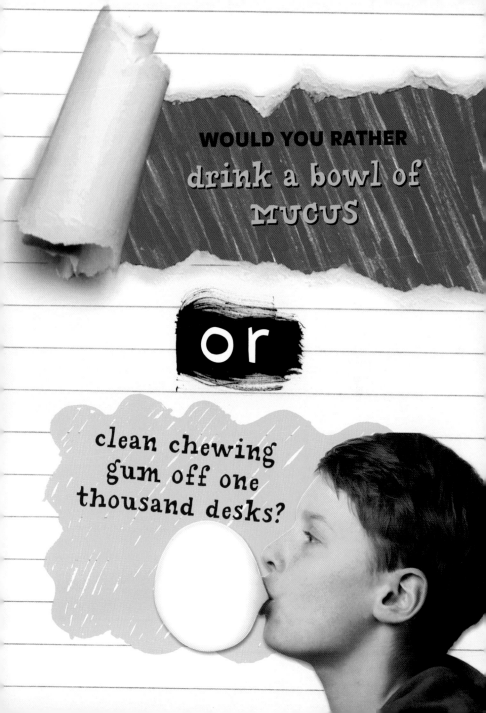

WOULD YOU RATHER

drink a bowl of
MUCUS

or

clean chewing
gum off one
thousand desks?

find out you're a clone

find out your future has already been decided?

WOULD YOU RATHER

go back a grade
in school

or

go up five grades
in school?

WOULD YOU RATHER

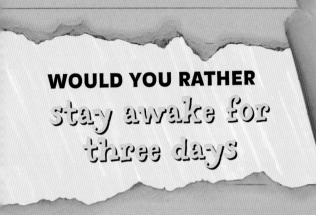

stay awake for three days

or

sleep through a very important test?

WOULD YOU RATHER be naked in front of your family

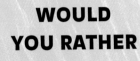

in front of a bunch of strangers who don't care?

WOULD YOU RATHER
stuff your mouth with marshmallows and give an hour-long speech

or

fill your pants with spaghetti and walk around the mall for an hour?

WOULD YOU RATHER
get lost in an unfamiliar country

or

fly a plane
by yourself?

WOULD YOU RATHER 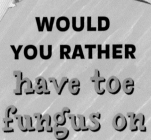 have toe fungus on your feet

 or

warts on your arms?

WOULD YOU RATHER drink a glass of milk someone washed their feet in

or

eat a bowl of macaroni that's been topped with snot?

WOULD YOU RATHER

talk in a whisper
so that people
constantly ask
you to repeat
yourself

only be able
to shout?

WOULD YOU RATHER

show up thirty minutes
early to school every day

or

show up
ten minutes late
to a big game you're
participating in?

WOULD YOU RATHER get trapped in a porta potty

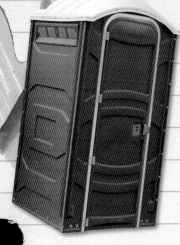

in a very crowded subway car pressed against a stinky stranger?

WOULD YOU RATHER

have one totally amazing and incredible birthday party once every five years

one poorly attended, sad birthday party once a year?

WOULD YOU RATHER
stick your hand in a clogged toilet

stick your
hand up the
butt of a
moose?

WOULD YOU RATHER

ask a stranger for help

or

have a stranger ask you for help?

WOULD YOU RATHER

start a fight with someone bigger than you

or

walk a tightrope between two skyscrapers?

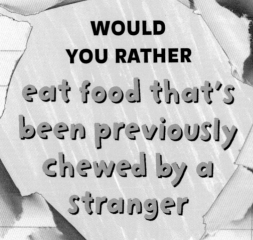

**WOULD
YOU RATHER**

eat food that's
been previously
chewed by a
stranger

or

food that's
been licked
up and down
by a camel?

WOULD YOU RATHER

have a
nose-hair
braid

an eyelash-hair
braid?

WOULD YOU RATHER
be the number one bowler
in the world

be a
member of a
number one
basketball
team?

WOULD YOU RATHER wake up shaking from a terrible nightmare

go to bed worried that someone is hiding in your closet?

WOULD YOU RATHER

drink a jar of **PICKLE JUICE**

or

rinse your mouth out with **SARDINES?**

WOULD YOU RATHER
find out your
mom is the
EVIL QUEEN
of a forgotten
world

that you're an
ALIEN?

WOULD YOU RATHER

sleep in a big pile of garbage

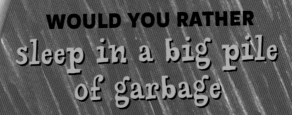

or

with a relative who is a notorious bed-wetter?

WOULD YOU RATHER sit in a **HOT CAR**

or

stand in a **FREEZER?**

WOULD YOU RATHER
have a friend who talks
behind your back

or

have a
friend who
makes up lies
to protect
themselves?

WOULD YOU RATHER

go to a movie
by yourself

or

exercise in
front of a large
audience?

WOULD YOU RATHER
have two gigantic front teeth that are the size of two stamps

one tooth that is brown from rot?

WOULD YOU RATHER

be covered in fuzzy pink hair

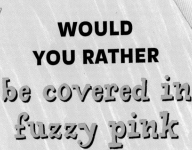

or

dance like a weirdo in front of your principal?

WOULD YOU RATHER

live as your
MOM for a day

live as your
DAD for a day?

WOULD YOU RATHER
listen to a baby scream for an hour

or

listen to someone you dislike talking nonstop about something you **HATE** for three hours?

WOULD YOU RATHER

find a mysterious check made out to you for **$100**

give **$1,000** to people in need?

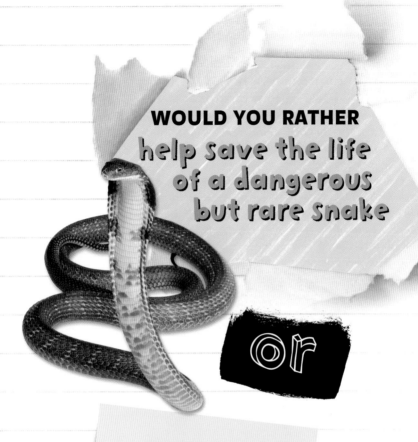

WOULD YOU RATHER
help save the life of a dangerous but rare snake

or

stick your hand in a lobster tank?

WOULD YOU RATHER
become an adult now

stay a kid for the rest of your life?

WOULD YOU RATHER
give up HUGS for a year

or

kiss a
gross old
TROLL?

WOULD YOU RATHER braid someone's toe hair

or

clean out a rabbit cage that's been unattended for months?

WOULD YOU RATHER

give your best friend an extra year of life

or

rescue a cute puppy?

WOULD YOU RATHER have gills, so you can **SWIM UNDERWATER**

have wings, so you can **FLY?**

WOULD YOU RATHER

chew a ball of BELLY BUTTON LINT

eat an EARWAX POPSICLE?

WOULD YOU RATHER
climb one thousand stairs to win a mystery prize

or

climb one hundred stairs for a pizza?

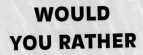

**WOULD
YOU RATHER**

write a very
important paper
with the wrong
hand

give a speech to
your class with
your eyes closed?

WOULD YOU RATHER

act like a baby for an entire day of school

dress like a baby for a week?

WOULD YOU RATHER leave the country forever

never ever leave the state you live in?

WOULD YOU RATHER sleep with a poisonous reptile every night

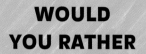

live in a bear cave for one month?

WOULD YOU RATHER

have large, floppy eyelids

have a super-gigantic head?

WOULD YOU RATHER

run a mile barefoot on a pathway made of jagged rocks

run a mile barefoot on smooth pavement that is hot to the touch?

WOULD YOU RATHER

tell a little lie in front
of one hundred people

or

tell a big lie
to only your
best friend?

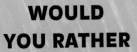

WOULD YOU RATHER have the ability to talk to a single animal

or

the ability to hear the spirits of the dead?

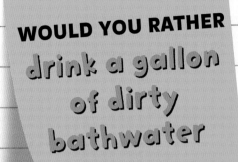

WOULD YOU RATHER
drink a gallon of dirty bathwater

or

drink one cup of dishwashing soap?

dish soap

WOULD YOU RATHER
have a body like a
TARANTULA'S

a huge,
BONY FIN
on your
back?

WOULD YOU RATHER

tell a big secret on
the nightly news

or

tell a small
secret to your
entire family?

WOULD YOU RATHER

continuously chew lemons for thirty minutes

or

drink a tub of barbeque sauce?

WOULD YOU RATHER spend the day swimming with a mermaid family

or

spend the day riding dragons?

WOULD YOU RATHER

hang out with
ONLY BOYS

or

hang out with
ONLY GIRLS?

WOULD YOU RATHER

your mom was very mad at you

very disappointed in you?

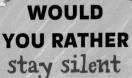

WOULD YOU RATHER stay silent when a friend gets in trouble for something they didn't do

or

take the blame for something they did?

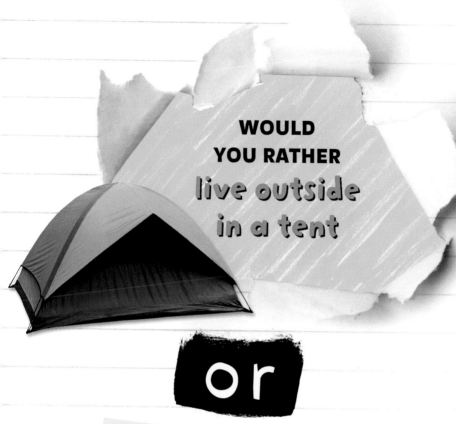

WOULD YOU RATHER live outside in a tent

or

live inside in a small closet?

WOULD YOU RATHER

have a ZIT popped right into your mouth

chew on a BLOODY SCAB?

WOULD YOU RATHER

eat a frozen platter
of MAC AND CHEESE

warm chocolate
ice cream with
PEAS?

WOULD YOU RATHER wear high-heeled shoes for five days

a damp bathing suit under your clothes for a week?

WOULD YOU RATHER

win a game versus a **NOVICE**

or

lose a game versus an **EXPERT?**

WOULD YOU RATHER
get stood up by your crush

or

find out your best friend lied to you?

WOULD YOU RATHER

be known for being
mean and nasty

or

for being
rude and
ignorant?

WOULD YOU RATHER
be known for being
a super-talented
TUBA PLAYER

an amazing
MACARONI ARTIST?

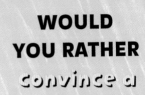

WOULD YOU RATHER convince a stranger that you are royalty in disguise

or

convince a stranger that a banana can be used as a phone?

WOULD YOU RATHER only be able to talk in gibberish to your crush

only be able to communicate with your family by pointing?

WOULD YOU RATHER **SPROUT WINGS**

develop
CLAW
HANDS?

**WOULD
YOU RATHER**
have someone
cough in your
face

or

sneeze in
your hair?

WOULD YOU RATHER

eat a hot dog covered in live caterpillars

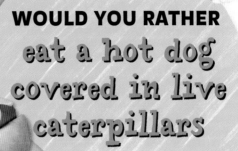

or

a burrito made with crickets?

WOULD YOU RATHER

wear a
Coat of
human hair

find a
Cockroach in
your salad?

WOULD YOU RATHER smell like ROTTEN EGGS

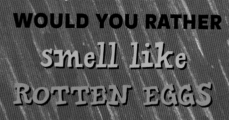

smell like a WET DOG?

WOULD YOU RATHER tickle an **ANGRY PIG**

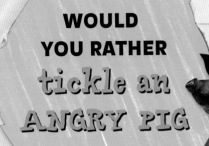

or

dance with a **DONKEY?**

WOULD YOU RATHER

find a hornets' nest in your closet

or

hundreds of baby spiders?

WOULD YOU RATHER
be trapped in a car
with a mean bully

or

with
someone who
can't stop
farting?

WOULD YOU RATHER

put your foot
in a mysterious
vibrating box

or

stick your
hand in a
beehive?

WOULD YOU RATHER

say, "Aw SHUCKS!"
every time someone pays
you a compliment

or

"MORNING, BABY
BOO-BOO BEAR!"
every time someone
greets you?

WOULD YOU RATHER learn how to fly an **AIRPLANE**

or

learn how to drive a **TRACTOR?**

WOULD YOU RATHER
have a COOL JOB
and no social life

or

have a really
BORING JOB
and an awesome
social life?

WOULD YOU RATHER
eat a bowl of thick, brown mustard

or

eat a salt-and-pepper sandwich with **LOTS** of salt and pepper?

WOULD YOU RATHER reveal your crush to your grandma

accidentally walk in on your brother in the shower?

WOULD YOU RATHER

wear wet socks for a month

sing **"HAPPY BIRTHDAY"** to no one in particular every hour on the hour for a week?

WOULD YOU RATHER get advice from a tiny DEVIL that is very sweet

or

from a mean little ANGEL?

WOULD YOU RATHER

wet your bed every night for a year

have a poop explosion in front of your class?

WOULD YOU RATHER

eat a taco filled with **BUG MEAT**

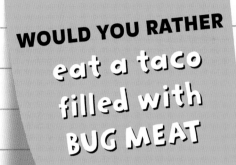

or

an omelet made with **OLD GRASS CLIPPINGS?**

WOULD YOU RATHER plan a **SURPRISE PARTY** for your least favorite teacher

or

improvise an **HOUR-LONG SPEECH** for a bunch of rowdy second graders?

WOULD YOU RATHER

live in a bustling city surrounded by people, noise, and lights

or

in a rural community that's very quiet and peaceful?

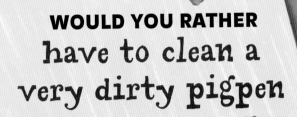

WOULD YOU RATHER have to clean a very dirty pigpen

or

paint your bedroom with a tiny paintbrush?

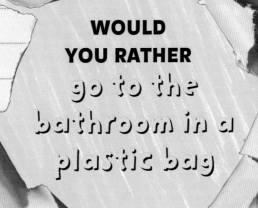

WOULD YOU RATHER go to the bathroom in a plastic bag

or

in a litter box?

WOULD YOU RATHER

wear a suit made of garbage

or

wear a bad wig and tell everyone you love it?

WOULD YOU RATHER
smell a horrible fart

hot and
stinky
breath?

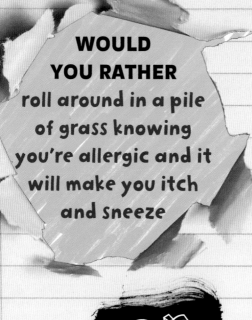

WOULD YOU RATHER roll around in a pile of grass knowing you're allergic and it will make you itch and sneeze

or

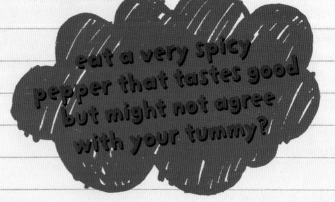

eat a very spicy pepper that tastes good but might not agree with your tummy?

WOULD YOU RATHER

shrink yourself down until you're an inch tall

grow yourself into a 100-foot-tall giant?

WOULD YOU RATHER

wear a shirt
that reads
**"I STEAL
STUFF"**
for a month

spend three
days in
JAIL?

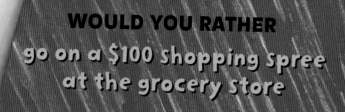

WOULD YOU RATHER
go on a $100 shopping spree
at the grocery store

or

buy one
very rare and
expensive
book?

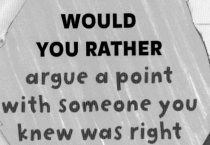

WOULD YOU RATHER argue a point with someone you knew was right

or

tell a person who made a mistake that they're actually correct?

WOULD YOU RATHER get chased by a bunch of strangers

or

chased by one person who is three times your size?

WOULD YOU RATHER

eat a big bucket of uncooked hot dogs

or

a basket of raw squid tentacles?

WOULD YOU RATHER
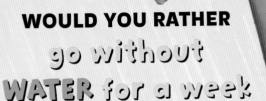
go without
WATER for a week

go without
VIDEO GAMES
for a month?

WOULD YOU RATHER unknowingly wear your underwear on the outside of your clothes all day long

have a runny nose you can't wipe for five hours?

know the exact moment you'll get your heart broken the worst

or

the exact moment you'll find out you were betrayed by someone you trust?

WOULD YOU RATHER

have a chip in your neck that tells your parents where you are at all times

or

be forced to watch a video of your parents yelling at one another?

WOULD YOU RATHER

totally forget your mom's birthday

find out you have a test at the very last minute with no time to prepare?

WOULD YOU RATHER watch a baseball game knowing you'll be hit in the face by a fly ball

sit in a slowly deflating raft in the middle of the ocean for ten hours?

WOULD YOU RATHER

camp in the middle of nowhere

or

spend the night in a haunted basement?

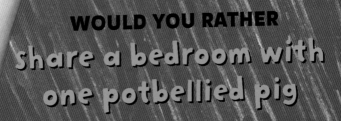

WOULD YOU RATHER
share a bedroom with
one potbellied pig

or

with
twenty-five
bunnies?

WOULD YOU RATHER have a tiny winged man as your best friend

possess the world's biggest diamond?

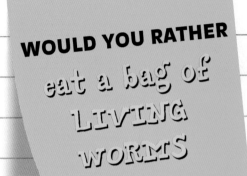

WOULD YOU RATHER

eat a bag of
LIVING
WORMS

eat one
DEAD RAT?

WOULD YOU RATHER
glue the fingers on your right hand together like a flipper

tie your legs together like a mermaid tail?

WOULD YOU RATHER

have a crush on a person who smells very bad

or

a person who treats others like dirt?

WOULD YOU RATHER

wear a hat filled with **BABY VOMIT**

wear a jacket worn by a **CORPSE?**

WOULD YOU RATHER add six more inches to your neck

or

walk like a gorilla?

WOULD YOU RATHER

give up candy forever

give up soda forever?

WOULD YOU RATHER

be on the news wearing a
frilly dress and clown makeup

dressed like a
wizard yelling,
**"THE RHYTHM
IS GONNA
GET YOU!"**

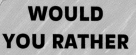

WOULD YOU RATHER eat roadkill for dinner every night for a year

or

never eat French fries ever again?

**WOULD
YOU RATHER**
live next to a
sewage treatment
plant

next to a
busy train
station?

WOULD YOU RATHER

have the best
Christmas ever
and get all the
gifts you wanted

give a nice
Christmas to a kid
who has never
had one?

WOULD YOU RATHER
have greasy hair
that's five feet long

or

a stomach
that never stops
grumbling?

WOULD YOU RATHER meet a famous person you idolize who turns out to be very mean

or

be forced to convince a very wealthy person to give you $100?

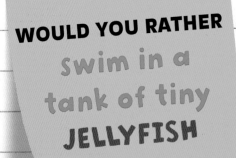

WOULD YOU RATHER

swim in a
tank of tiny
JELLYFISH

or

sleep in a crib
with a **SCORPION?**

WOULD YOU RATHER

swim in a kiddie pool filled with **ROTTEN VEGETABLES**

smell like **PEPPERONI** for a week?